Searchlight BOOKS™

What's Cool
about Science?

Discover

Nanotechnology

Lisa J. Amstutz

Lerner Publications ◆ Minneapolis

Content Consultant: Na Li, Postdoctoral Researcher, Nanotech Institute, The University of Texas at Dallas

Lerner Publications Company
A division of Lerner Publishing Group, Inc.

241 First Avenue North
Minneapolis, MN 55401 USA

For reading levels and more information, look up this title at
www.lernerbooks.com.

Library of Congress Cataloging-in-Publication Data

Names: Amstutz, Lisa J., author.
Title: Discover nanotechnology / by Lisa J. Amstutz.
Description: Minneapolis : Lerner Publications, [2017] | Series: Searchlight books. What's cool about science? | Audience: Ages 8–11. | Audience: Grades 4 to 6. | Includes bibliographical references and index.
Identifiers: LCCN 2016003150 (print) | LCCN 2016008021 (ebook) | ISBN 9781512408065 (lb : alk. paper) | ISBN 9781512412888 (pb : alk. paper) | ISBN 9781512410679 (eb pdf)
Subjects: LCSH: Nanotechnology—Juvenile literature.
Classification: LCC T174.7 .A56 2017 (print) | LCC T174.7 (ebook) | DDC 620.5—dc23

LC record available at http://lccn.loc.gov/2016003150

Manufactured in the United States of America
1 – VP – 7/15/16

Contents

Chapter 1
WHAT IS NANOTECHNOLOGY? ... **page 4**

Chapter 2
WORKING AT THE NANOSCALE ... **page 12**

Chapter 3
USING NANOTECHNOLOGY ... **page 18**

Chapter 4
CONCERNS ABOUT NANOTECHNOLOGY ... **page 30**

Glossary • 38
Learn More about Nanotechnology • 39
Index • 40

WHAT IS NANOTECHNOLOGY?

Nanotechnology is the science of very small things. Everything in the world, from the hair on a person's head to the plastic in a lunch tray, is made up of tiny parts. These parts are called molecules.

Everything you see here, including lunch trays, food, and people, is made up of molecules. What are molecules made up of?

Molecules are made up of even smaller parts called atoms. Atoms are so small they can only be seen with a powerful microscope. Things around the size of molecules and atoms are called nanomaterials. They range from 1 to 100 nanometers in size.

Because atoms and molecules are so difficult to see, people often use models when learning about them.

How Small Is a Nanometer?

It's hard to imagine how small a nanometer is. It is one billionth of a meter. A human hair is about 100,000 nanometers wide. Each page in this book is about 100,000 nanometers thick!

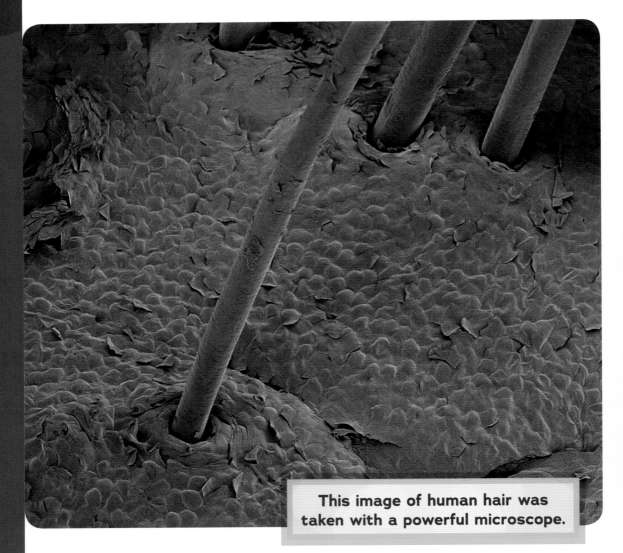

This image of human hair was taken with a powerful microscope.

A nanomaterial may be 1 to 100 nanometers wide in one direction. It may be much larger in another direction. One example of this is the carbon nanotube. This nanomaterial is made up of carbon atoms. They are assembled into a tube shape. The tube may be 1 nanometer or less wide, but millions of nanometers long.

This illustration of a carbon nanotube shows individual carbon atoms as black spheres.

The History of Nanotechnology

The idea of nanotechnology came from a 1959 talk by physicist Richard Feynman. He said that someday, scientists would be able to move atoms around. That sounded like an impossible dream.

Feynman went on to win the Nobel Prize in Physics in 1965.

Scanning tunneling microscopes work by scanning a sample with a sharp-tipped object called a stylus. The tip of the stylus is just one atom wide.

But just twenty-two years later, that dream came true. In 1981, the scanning tunneling microscope was invented. It let scientists see single atoms and molecules. A tiny probe on the machine allowed scientists to move these particles around.

The shape of peacock feathers at the nano scale breaks up light and reflects it back in striking colors.

Applying Nanotechnology

Nature already uses nanomaterials. Lotus plants have self-cleaning leaves. Bones have nanoscale structures that help make them strong and light. Butterflies and peacocks get their vivid colors from nanostructures.

Science is just beginning to unlock the possibilities of artificial nanotechnology. It's difficult to work with such tiny things. But that hasn't stopped people from doing it. Many common products are made with nanotechnology. Tennis balls, clothing, and sunscreen are a few examples. Nanotechnology helps tennis balls last longer. It prevents clothing from getting stained. It makes sunscreen more effective. This field of science has brought new materials and structures from imagination into reality.

Nanotech coatings inside a tennis ball stop air from escaping, helping the ball keep its bounce over time.

Chapter 2

WORKING AT THE NANOSCALE

One problem with working at the nanoscale is finding the right tools. It's hard to work with materials the human eye can't see! Advanced microscopes have probes that can move single atoms a short distance. But what if a scientist wanted to move many of them?

Building structures at the nanoscale, such as these gears, requires special tools. What is one tool scientists use to move atoms?

In a nanotechnology lab, scientists use different tools to move atoms. For example, they use spinners and evaporators to lay down thin layers of nanoparticles. They use light-sensitive chemicals to make patterns with nanostructures. They use sprayers, ovens, and dryers to coat objects in nanomaterials. Layers, patterns, and coatings made of nanoparticles can give objects new properties and effects. They change the way the object's surface interacts with its environment.

This device coats drill bits with a nanomaterial that makes them stronger.

Some of the work is done in a clean room. This room is dust-free. Its temperature and humidity are carefully controlled. If they are too high or too low, they could change the way particles behave. People working in the clean room must wear masks, gloves, and special suits. With tiny nanoparticles, even a tiny hair or a stray breath could cause problems.

This clean room is located in a research center in Finland.

RESEARCHERS USE LARGE PIECES OF CARBON, IN THE FORM OF THE MINERAL GRAPHITE, TO CREATE NANODIAMONDS.

Engineers make new nanomaterials in two ways. The first is by breaking down materials into smaller parts. For example, large pieces of carbon can be broken down into tiny diamonds called nanodiamonds.

The second way to make nanomaterials is to build them from even smaller parts. Individual atoms are combined to form nanoparticles. Scientists are looking for other ways to make nanomaterials. One idea is to create materials that build themselves when the right parts are put near each other. This is called self-assembling.

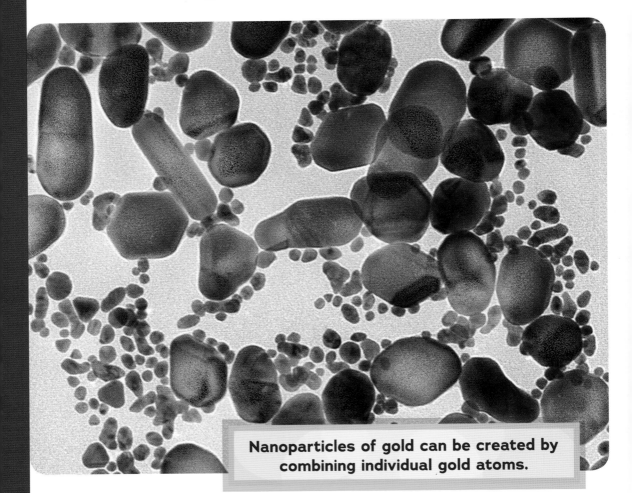

Nanoparticles of gold can be created by combining individual gold atoms.

Building with Nanocars

Scientists have designed a car made entirely from one molecule. Scientists arranged individual atoms into a carlike shape. A nanocar is about one billionth the size of a real car. Its tiny wheels can spin. Electricity powers the car. In the future, nanocars could be used to move atoms and molecules around. They could even be used to build computer parts.

This illustration shows a nanocar moving along a surface of gold atoms.

Chapter 3

USING NANOTECHNOLOGY

Someday, nanotechnology may help save lives. Scientists are working on ways to use nanotechnology in the field of medicine. Many of these advances are already being tested on lab animals.

This thin, flexible medical sensor is made possible by nanotechnology. How is medical nanotechnology often tested?

Perhaps one day nanoscale robots, known as nanobots, will travel through the body to find and fix problems. They may deliver medicine, clear blocked arteries, and help repair injuries.

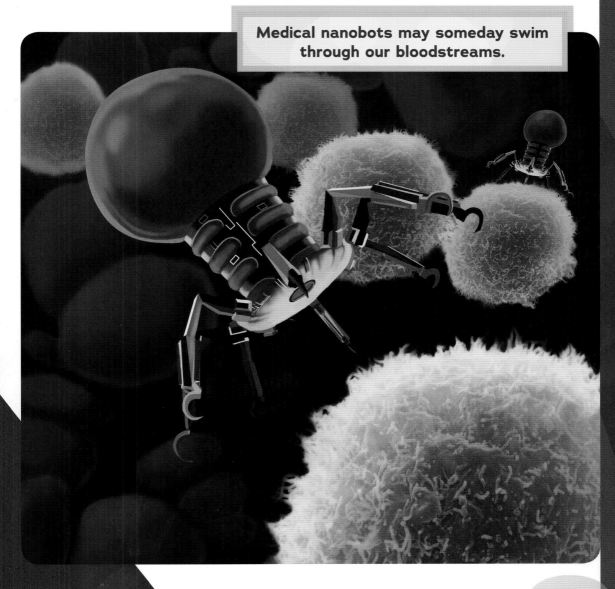

Medical nanobots may someday swim through our bloodstreams.

One type of nanoparticle that shows promise in fighting cancer is called a dendrimer. It has tiny branches all over it. Scientists can attach vitamins to some of the branches. Then they stick an anticancer drug on the rest. Cancer cells attract the vitamins. When the cancer cells pull the dendrimer inside, the anticancer drug kills them.

The many branches of dendrimers give them a large surface area for their size.

An Australian company introduced this water-resistant nanotechnology fabric in 2014.

Cleaning with Nanotechnology

Nanotechnology can make everyday items stay clean. For example, special coatings on glass make windows clean themselves when it rains. The water spreads out and rinses away dirt as it runs off. Other coatings make water and dirt roll off fabric.

Nanotechnologies that use waxy surfaces to repel water work the same way that lotus leaves do in nature.

There are two ways to use nanotechnology to make surfaces self-cleaning. The first is to create a waxy coating with tiny bumps. Water and dirt cannot stick to the bumps very well.

Another type of coating works in the opposite way. It fills in tiny cracks to make the surface extra smooth. Then water spreads out in a thin film rather than forming beads. It carries dirt away as it slides off.

Some water-resistant nanotechnology coatings can even be used to protect phones if they are dunked under water.

Nanosilver

Nanotechnology can even be found in shampoo. A substance called nanosilver is used in some shampoos to keep them from spoiling. It can also be found in some socks, sheets, and stuffed animals. It stops harmful bacteria from growing.

Nanosilver has been used in products such as yoga mats, combs, and food containers.

Since ancient times, people have used silver to treat wounds. But nanosilver kills bacteria even better than regular silver. Since nanosilver is made up of so many tiny particles, it has a large surface area. This lets it give off more ions than regular silver. These ions kill the bacteria.

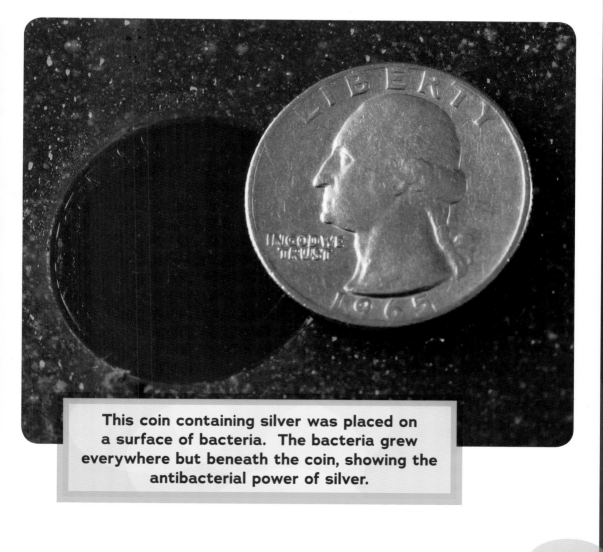

This coin containing silver was placed on a surface of bacteria. The bacteria grew everywhere but beneath the coin, showing the antibacterial power of silver.

Food, Water, and Nanotech

Nanotechnology can also be found in the kitchen. Nanotech containers keep drinks from losing their fizz. Tiny particles of clay help seal the glass so carbon dioxide cannot escape. Nanoclay can also be used in plastic containers to keep water and oxygen out. This keeps dry snacks such as nuts fresh longer.

Nanotechnology can help keep drinks fizzier for longer before they are poured and enjoyed.

Powering Up

Some nanomaterials make fuel burn more cleanly and efficiently. Their small size gives them extra surface area. They can react with more chemicals at once. When they are added to automobile fuel, more of the fuel is used up. Less air pollution is created.

This researcher is working on cerium oxide nanotubes, one of the nanomaterials that may improve automobile fuels.

Nanomaterials may help solar panels work better in the future, too. Today's solar cells capture only 10 to 20 percent of the sunlight that hits them. Researchers are working on ways to use nanomaterials to trap more energy.

THIS EXPERIMENTAL SOLAR CELL IS COVERED IN BILLIONS OF NANOWIRES.

Nanotubes to Space?

NASA and other groups are working on designs for a space elevator made from carbon nanotubes. A Japanese firm plans to build one by 2050. If built, the elevator could lift a spacecraft into outer space without using a huge rocket and lots of fuel. Carbon nanotubes are a hundred times stronger than steel of the same weight. The problem is figuring out how to make them long enough.

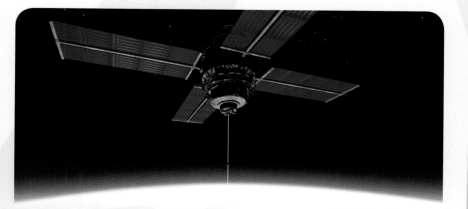

This artist's image shows one possible design for a space elevator. The elevator, visible as a thin white line, ends at a space station.

Chapter 4

CONCERNS ABOUT NANOTECHNOLOGY

Nanotechnology has lots of positive uses. But like any technology, it has downsides as well. Nanotechnology could be used to harm people. And scientists still aren't certain how it will affect human health and the environment. More studies are needed to make sure that nanotechnology is safe.

Researchers are working to make nanotechnology not only useful, but also safe. What are two things researchers are studying its effects on?

Gray Goo?

An engineer named Eric Drexler came up with the idea of making molecules that could create more of themselves. This would be useful in oil spills, for instance. Nanobots could break down the oil. Then they could use the oil to make more copies of themselves until it was all cleaned up.

Eric Drexler speaks about nanotechnology at a 2011 conference.

But what if the nanobots didn't stop there? What if they started gobbling up seawater, fish, and anything else they could find?

This artist's image shows a swarm of nanobots that can build copies of themselves.

Some oil spills are cleaned up using chemicals sprayed from boats. Nanobots may make such cleanups easier in the future.

Drexler worried they could turn everything on the planet into "gray goo." It sounds like a scene from a horror movie. Scientists take this concern seriously, though most have come to realize it is very unlikely.

Health Risks

Nanomaterials do not always act the same way larger materials do. Chemicals that are normally safe can become dangerous at the nanoscale. Some can slip through the skin into the body. Others can cause lung damage when they are inhaled. Still others can enter and damage the liver, heart, and brain. People who work with nanomaterials are at high risk. They need to wear safety gear.

This jar is filled with carbon nanotubes. If they enter the lungs, carbon nanotubes can cause cancer.

Many products now use nanotechnology, including this water-resistant spray. These products require testing to ensure safety.

Because nanotechnology is so new, there are not many laws about it yet. New products need lots of testing to make sure they are safe.

A Nanotech Future

Nanotechnology is here to stay. Scientists are working together to make it safe for the public. They will ensure it will be used for good and not for harm.

Scientists are creating new nanotech products every day. Perhaps one day people across the world will have nanotech solar cells built into their roofs. They may drink water cleaned with carbon nanotubes. Nanotechnology may even help them live longer. The future of this field is bright.

These scientists are investigating nanoscale droplets of liquid metal. Nanotechnology researchers are making discoveries that will change our world.

Invisibility

The invisibility cloak from the Harry Potter books may be closer to reality than you think. Scientists are working to create "invisible" fabric. Nanoparticles in the fabric will reflect light like mirrors. This will make the object the fabric covers appear invisible.

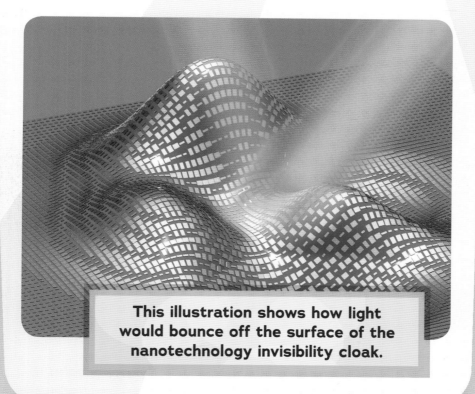

This illustration shows how light would bounce off the surface of the nanotechnology invisibility cloak.

Glossary

atom: the basic building block of matter

ion: an atom or molecule with a positive or negative charge

molecule: a small unit of matter made up of a group of atoms bonded together

nanobot: a nanoscale robot

nanomaterial: particles, crystals, and other materials that are used to build nanoscale products

nanometer: a billionth of a meter

nanoparticle: a particle measuring between 1 and 100 nanometers in size in at least one direction

Learn More about Nanotechnology

Books

Heinrichs, Ann. *Cool Science Careers: Nanotechnologist.* Ann Arbor, MI: Cherry Lake Publishing, 2009. Read about how nanotechnologists use tiny bits of matter to create new products.

Piddock, Charles. *Future Tech: From Personal Robots to Motorized Monocycles.* Washington, DC: National Geographic, 2009. Learn how nanotechnology and other new technologies may change our lives in the future.

Swanson, Jennifer. *Super Gear: Nanotechnology and Sports Team Up.* Watertown, MA: Charlesbridge, 2016. Discover how nanotechnology is used to create high-tech sports gear.

Websites

It's a Small World
http://www.ndep.us/its-a-small-world
Watch a video about the work that goes on in a nanotechnology lab.

Nanotechnology for Kids
http://www.explainthatstuff.com/nanotechnologyforkids.html
Learn more about the history and possible future of nanotechnology.

Nanozone
http://nanozone.org
Read about the scientists who are developing today's nanotechnology.

Index

atoms, 5, 7, 8–9, 12–13, 16, 17

carbon nanotubes, 7, 29, 36

cleaning nanotechnology, 21–23

clean rooms, 14

dangers, 30–35

Drexler, Eric, 31, 33

Feynman, Richard, 8

invisibility, 37

medical nanotechnology, 18–20

microscopes, 5, 9, 12

molecules, 4–5, 9, 17, 31

nanobots, 19, 31–32

nanocars, 17

nanomaterials, 5, 7, 10, 13, 15–16, 27–28, 34

nanosilver, 24–25

nanotechnology tools, 13

solar panels, 28

space elevator, 29

Photo Acknowledgments

The images in this book are used with the permission of: © Highwaystarz-Photography/iStock.com, p. 4; © Xavier Arnau/iStock.com, p. 5; © David Scharf/Science Source, p. 6; © PaulFleet/iStock.com, p. 7; © Estate of Francis Bello/Science Source, p. 8; © Science Source, pp. 9, 27, 36; © martinwimmer/iStock.com, p. 10; © Pavlo_K/iStock.com, p. 11; © Volker Steger/Science Source, pp. 12, 28; © RIA Novosti/Science Source, p. 13; © AIRIO/REX/Newscom, p. 14; © Tyler Boyes/Shutterstock.com, p. 15; © David McCarthy/Science Source, p. 16; © James Tour, Rice University, p. 17; © Yoshikazu Tsuno/AFP/Getty Images, p. 18; © Spencer Sutton/Science Source, p. 19; © Hybrid Medical Animation/Science Source, p. 20; © Threadsmiths/Lewis Pitchford/REX/AP Images, p. 21; © CreativaImages/iStock.com, p. 22; © Edgar Su/Reuters, p. 23; © Bill Hogan/Chicago Tribune/MCT/Newscom, p. 24; © Scimat/Science Source, p. 25; © warongdech/iStock.com, p. 26; © Victor Habbick Visions/Science Photo Library/Newscom, p. 29; © Andrew Brookes/National Physical Laboratory/Science Source, p. 30; © Sergei Ilnitsky/EPA/Newscom, p. 31; © Victor Habbick Visions/Science Source, p. 32; © Chris Hellier/Science Source, p. 33; © Pat Sullivan/AP Images, p. 34; © GH1/NeverWet & Nathan Sharratt/WENN/Newscom, p. 35; © Xinhua/Xinhua Press/Corbis, p. 37.

Front Cover: © Paul Wootton/Science Source.

Main body text set in Adrianna Regular 14/20.
Typeface provided by Chank.